N… …ppies

…ld

ill… …d by Pamela Venus

CW01652673

Published by Dinosaur Publications

Anna is a big girl now.
She can do lots of things
babies can't do.
She can climb stairs.

She can drink milk
from a cup.
She can draw pictures.

She can pull on her boots.
And she can go to the potty,
all by herself.

P. VENUS

Once Anna wore nappies.
When she peed or made a poo,
she did it in her nappy.

Sometimes she makes a poo too.
Then she wipes her bottom with paper.
Sometimes her Mummy helps her.

She pulls up her pants.
She empties the potty.
She washes her hands.
And she is ready to play.

Anna is the only one who knows
when it's time for her
to go to the potty. Sometimes,
when she's outside playing,
she doesn't want to go.
It's more fun to play
than to go to the potty.
But wet pants spoil the fun.

So to keep her pants dry,
Anna runs to the potty.
Sometimes she doesn't get
there in time.
But usually she does.

Big girls learn
to do lots of things.
They can learn to ride a tricycle,
comb their hair,
and go down the slide.
Learning to use a potty
is one more way of
becoming a big girl.

Text copyright © Maryann Macdonald 1980
Illustrations copyright © Pamela Venus 1988
Published by Dinosaur Publications
8 Grafton Street, London W1X 3LA

Dinosaur Publications is an imprint
of the Children's Division, part
of the Collins Publishing Group

Printed by Warners of Bourne and London